The Western Lancet, June 1877: A Monthly
Journal Of Clinical Medicine And Surgery

University Of California

In the interest of creating a more extensive selection of rare historical book reprints, we have chosen to reproduce this title even though it may possibly have occasional imperfections such as missing and blurred pages, missing text, poor pictures, markings, dark backgrounds and other reproduction issues beyond our control. Because this work is culturally important, we have made it available as a part of our commitment to protecting, preserving and promoting the world's literature. Thank you for your understanding.

CONTENTS.
JUNE, 1877.

ORIGINAL COMMUNICATIONS—
Case of Strangulated Inguinal Hernia of 4 days and 18 hours Standing; Operation; Recovery. By W. F. Miller, M. D., - 133
Cosmoline as an Excipient in Diseases of the Skin. By Alfred Emanuel Regensburger, M. D., - 135
Case of Brain Fever, with Treatment. By W. A. Goddard, M. D., - 136–138

EXTRACTS—
Radical Treatment of Uterine Cancer, - 139
Treatment of Sebaceous Tumors, - 140
Ulcer of the Stomach, - 141
Epithelioma of Neck of Uterus Cured by Five Injections of a Solution of Chloride of Zinc, - 141
Medical Education at Philadelphia, - 142
Local Anesthesias Cured by Metals, - 143
Early Sign of Phthisis, - 143
Safe and Rapid Cure for Aneurism, - 144
Treatment of Acute Pneumonia by Turpentine, - 144
Evolution of the Placenta, - 145
Careless Prescribing, - 145
Treatment of Granular Lids by Acetate of Lead, - 146

MEDICAL NOTES—
German Law in Regard to Second Dispensing of Prescriptions, - 146

COMMUNICATIONS—
The Assault upon upon Dr. G. G. Tyrrell, - 147

EDITORIAL—
Medical Department of University of Pennsylvania, - 148
Russian Imperial Technical Society and Metric Weights and Measures, - 148
Chlorine vs. Carbolic Acid in Surgery, - 149

BOOK REVIEWS—
Report on Medical Education, to the Medical Society of California. By Arthur B. Stout, M. D., - 150
Transactions of the American Gynæcological Society. Vol. I. - 151
Cyclopædia of the Practice of Medicine. By Dr. H. Von Ziemssen, - 152
Atlas of Skin Diseases. By Louis A. Duhring, M. D., - 152
Transactions of the N. Y. Pathological Society, - 153

HEALTH REPORTS—
Report of Deaths in Sacramento City, month of May, 1877, - 154
Report of Deaths and their Causes in the State during February, 1877, - 155
Report of Deaths in San Francisco during May, 1877, - 156

FLEMMING & TALBOT,
814 Filbert Street,   Philadelphia, Pa.

MANUFACTURERS OF AND DEALERS IN

Electro-Medical Instruments
AND
BATTERIES.

Having largely increased their manufacturing facilities, they are now prepared to furnish the most improved Portable and Permanent Batteries for use in Electro-Therapeutics and Galvano-Cautery.

SEND FOR CATALOGUE.

J. H. A. FOLKE
No. 118 Montgomery Street,
Agents for the Pa

THE WESTERN LANCET:

A JOURNAL OF

CLINICAL MEDICINE AND SURGERY.

Original Communications.

Case of Strangulated Inguinal Hernia of 4 Days and 18 Hours Standing; Operation; Recovery.

BY W. F. MILLER, M. D., HILL'S FERRY, CAL.

On the evening of the 28th of April, 1877, I was called to see C. Gurtz, in great haste. On examining him I found him suffering excruicatingly from strangulated hernia. I shall give his own words as related to me on my examination: "Some four days ago, I was about 60 miles from here engaged in hauling a load of wool, and while preparing a camp-fire — in a kneeling posture—the trouble occurred. I was seized with great pain and vomiting. I tried to put it back myself, but having no one near but a boy, and being far away from any house where I could get help, I failed. I could get it back to a certain extent, then my strength gave out. I was troubled twice this way before, the last time twelve years ago, but it was put back in a few hours."

The tumor was about the size of a turkey egg. The surrounding parts were very much swollen and inflamed, the testicle was also swollen to twice its natural size, abdomen very tense, a great deal of tympanitis being present. Vomiting continually when any water or food was given; hiccough and severe pain were exhausting his strength very fast. The next morning the patient being etherized, an incision was made in a direct line upon the tumor about three inches long, each layer being carefully cut, the vessels were secured, and very little hemorrhage followed. The tumor being brought to view, was found to be very tense, highly congested, with small, dark spots upon the superior surface which had all the appearance of gangrene. I was advised by my assistant to make an artificial anus, to which I objected, and an exploring needle being introduced into the intestines through one of the apparently gangrenous spots, a slight hemorrhage followed. To make certain that this hemorrhage came from the walls of the intestines and not from the tumor itself a hypodermic syringe was introduced through the same opening. A quantity of clear fluid and gas was withdrawn, which relieved the tension of the tumor; nor was it refilled, showing that constriction was very great Then a light solution of perchloride of iron and glycerine was applied to the opening and the hemorrhage controlled. I concluded that there was vitality enough in the incarcerated loop of intestine to return it. The stricture being divided with great care, the adhesions which had formed at the external portion of the ring were broken up and a small portion of omentum removed. The intestine was then returned. After the wound was carefully cleansed, the edges were brought together with silver sutures, with a piece of lint left in the wound for drainage. A dressing of cosmoline ointment of salicylic acid 10 gr to 1 ʒ, and over all a cold carbolated water compress, the whole being secured by a bandage. The patient soon rallied from the shock and felt a little easier, with the exception of hiccough which made him suffer severely at times, for which I gave him tincture aconite rad gtt IV Hoffman's anodyne ʒ 1, which relieved him. The following treatment was kept up for the first five days. Quiniæ grs ii., lactopeptine, grs ii., morphine grs ¼ every 4 hours: beef tea every hour; whiskey, a teaspoonful every 2 hours; turpentine stupes; Indian meal and flax seed poultices over the abdomen. At 6 P. M. the bowels moved spontaneously and discharged a large quantity of black fæces, which gave the patient the greatest relief. At 8 P. M. the hiccough stopped entirely and he slept for hours. In the morning he was much better. The following is the table of pulse and temperature for the first five days: April 29th, pulse 100, temperature 101; 30th, pulse 100, temperature, 99; May 1st, pulse 100, temperature 101; 2d, pulse 88 temperature 98; 3d, pulse 90, temperature 98½; after which the pulse and temperature did not vary very much from their normal standard. After this the powders were not given so often; the bowels moved without any trouble every second or third day. No unpleasant symptoms followed during the entire course. The inflammation being controlled, soon subsided, and nature's reparation proceeded without interruption, and twenty-nine days after the operation the wound had entirely closed and the patient walked with ease and comfort.

Cosmoline as an Excipient in Diseases of the Skin.

BY ALFRED EMANUEL REGENSBURGER, M. D.

In treating diseases of the skin, the most trifling matter often retards or interferes with the success of an otherwise judicious and excellent plan of treatment. Every dermatologist has frequently had occasion to observe that an ointment containing the same active ingredients, and in the same proportion, does real harm when one excipient is used, and is often of most decided advantage where another is substituted.

From the tenor of the above, the propriety of what follows becomes apparent at once: When I arrived in San Francisco I employed the usual officinal ointments, which nearly all contain lard as a basis, and had recourse also to this substance, for the same purpose, in many of my own formulæ. As a matter of course, I expected to obtain the same results from them, under analogous circumstances, as in the East. In this regard my expectation was not realized. At first I was unable to account for it. A more extended inquiry led me to believe that it could be explained by the greater proneness of California lard to turn rancid, and its more irritating character than the Eastern article. To obviate these defects I intended using vaseline or romaline, which were introduced and used with a good deal of success by Professor Piffard, during the last few years in Charity Hospital, New York. These two substances not being procurable in San Francisco, I thought of trying another article of a similar nature, also a petroleum product — cosmoline — and I was gratified to see it fill all requirements so well, answering in many cases where lard could not be used. From that time I have used it with uniform success. As the result of my experience, I am convinced that it deserves to be more extensively employed as an excipient instead of lard, and I would suggest to physicians to give it a trial after a lard ointment has disappointed, before jumping from one ointment to another with the same barren results, ending, perhaps, in discouragement and failure.

Vancouver, Washington Territory, May 11, 1877.

Dr. R. A. McLean:

Dear Sir:—In accordance with your request, I send you the report of a case of Brain Fever. The patient was a boy seven years of age, living in Vancouver at that time (1866, and about the 27th of May, as near as I can remember). Two days before I saw the patient he had been treated by another physician. I did not acquaint myself with his treatment of the case specifically, but he pronounced the case hopeless, as there was no abatement of the fever. The boy was insensible to such a degree that he could recognize no one, and to all appearances hastening to his decease. I have forgotten the frequency of his pulse. I ordered hot water, a tub, towels and cloths, which were in readiness by the time an attendant could remove the mustard from his feet and legs and place a wet cloth upon the back of his neck where the mustard had produced vesication. I then placed him in the bath at 100° Fahrenheit, wetting his head with cold water, and holding his body erect in a sitting posture. In about one or two minutes, as soon as I saw that the skin indicated a return of the blood to the surface, I removed him from the tub put clothes wrung from warm water around his body, *cold* cloths to his head, and wrapped his feet in flannels, wrung out of hot water, and had dry blankets placed closely over all except his head. This was accomplished in the space of five minutes from the time he entered the bath. The patient then, for the first, recognized his parents. I succeeded in having him sleep in ten minutes more. The remainder of the treatment up to Sunday morning was simply to meet indications by keeping the head cool and attending to any fever symptoms by sponging or applying wet cloths if necessary. As the case was a serious one, I did not leave this for a nurse to attend to, but staid by the patient during the day and a good portion of the night. Thus passed Friday afternoon and night, Saturday and Saturday night. Sunday morning he wanted to eat and I allowed him to have eggs. This I should not have allowed nor any other solid food. All day long I observed him growing more and more talkative, until at last he became delirious and so pugnacious that he would swear at some playmate that he supposed was playing with him. I now ordered hot water, and at five o'clock P. M. put him through the same treatment as on Friday afternoon, but no reaction followed. In a moment I decided what to do. The father assisted me, and in about fifteen minutes after the bath I removed every wet cloth and directed the father to rub his body while I attended to his feet and legs; the object to be attained was to drive to blood *from* the head and viscera *to* the surface and extremities. This was accomplished in about three quarters of an hour; not by harsh rubbing and chafing of the skin, but by a light and rapid stroke of the surface. When all the moisture from the water appliances was gone and a nice glow established on the surface. I then wrapped him in dry blankets, put dry flannels around his feet, with warm bricks, wrapped to prevent burning, to the feet also. I directed the attendants for the night to preserve perfect silence and allow no light to shine upon his face while he slept; to keep his head cool by sponging, unless it became necessary to apply the compress; that in case the patient did not sleep, but seemed to grow worse, they would call me. The patient rested well, and the next few days was treated to wheat meal gruel, as he should have been from the first, on Sabbath morning. At twelve o'clock on Tuesday I dismissed the case. It may be observed that in this case there was no focal point of inflammation. Had such been the case, recovery would have been rendered doubly doubtful.

Truly yours,

W. A. GODDARD, M. D.

The Vienna papers of April 23d contain a telegram to the effect that Professor Billroth has gone to St. Petersburg. The fact is, he went unexpectedly to Kischenew, in Roumania on the Russian border, leaving word with no one as to his destination or length of stay. The supposition is that his mission is in the interest of the Russian hospital service, as Kischenew is a base of operations of the Russian army.

New Treatment for Burns.—Nitsche recommends the following application to burns. The whole burnt surface is painted thick and repeatedly with linseed oil containing salicylic acid in the proportion of one to ten. The surface is then covered with thick layers of Brun's batting and fastened with calico. The burned surface should not be previously washed; it should only be freed from the grossest uncleanliness and epidermis shreds. Suppuration is entirely avoided. *The Cincinnati Lancet and Observer.*

Extracts.

On the Radical Treatment of Uterine Cancer.—Professor Goodell, of the University of Pennsylvania, believes that it is not only often impossible but is clinically needless to distinguish *intra vitam* the various kinds of uterine cancer. He believes that cancer of the uterus is of all cancers the least prone to infect the system; its victims die not so much from specific systemic poisoning, and from transference to distant organs, as from septicæmia, from embolism, and from the exhaustion induced by pain, sleeplessness, and the bloody or serous fluxes. In cancer of the cervix the indications are either to eradicate the disease or, failing in this, to check the excessive discharges, to correct the fœtor and to allay the pain, and thus to prolong life. To effect this he advises removal of the cervix either by the écraseur or galvanic cautery. When the entire cancerous mass is not removed by these means, the remaining outgrowths and the underlying infiltrated tissues must be dug out with the finger-nails, scraped off with Simon's spoons or snipped off with scissors. The resulting deep and funnel-shaped cavity must next be cauterized with fuming nitric acid or the hot iron. This may be done either at the time of the operation or after an interval of a week or so. During the operation, if scraping be needful, the hemorrhage is usually quite free, but in Professor Goodell's experience it has always yielded to an injection of one part of Monsel's solution to three of water, followed by a sponge tampon lightly packed into the funnel-shaped pit. After the operation there is sharp fever for four and twenty hours or more. On the third or fourth day the discharges sometimes become offensive, and continue so for several days. After the scraping process the stench is invariably overpowering, and must be met by injections of a solution of permanganate of potash, and by large doses of quinine to guard against blood-poisoning.

In all his cases Professor Goodell enforces sexual abstinence, and orders the patients iron and bichloride of mercury as a tonic, arsenic to repress the tendency to reproduction of the new growth, and ergot to diminish the supply of blood to the uterus. He has now operated on thirteen cases, in all of which life was lengthened and made bearable; in one instance, as he believes, saved for good. The hemorrhages were stayed, the putrid discharges checked, the pains allayed, and the appetite restored, and bed-ridden patients were enabled to get up and resume their household avocations. Even when the womb was fixed by the extension of the disease to parts beyond operative reach, much was gained by removing all of the cancer that could be reached. The complexion invariably cleared up after the operation, and this fact leads Professor Goodell to think that the so-called cancerous cachexia is due not to a cancerous diathesis, but to absorption from a local cancerous deposit.

Injury to the peritoneum cannot always be avoided during the operation. Karl Braun, however, does not hesitate to include a portion of the peritoneum in order that the hot wire may pass through perfectly healthy tissue. He says he has repeatedly in this way opened into the peritoneal cavity without harm to the patients. In one case, while scraping with the finger nails, Professor Goodell opened into Douglas's cul-de-sac. No vaginal injections were used, no untoward symptoms arose.—*Medical and Surgical Reporter.*

Treatment of Sebaceous Tumors.—Dr. B. Hamilton, from the success which he has had in its use, recommends the employment of strong tincture of iodine in the treatment of those tumors. No bad effects follow the injection and no scar remains in the former site of the growth. The following points are of importance: 1. Make the puncture with a sharp pointed bistoury. The aperture should be no larger than is necessary to allow the escape of the contents of the tumor, and the admission of the nozzle of the syringe. 2. Empty the cyst of its entire contents. 3. Distend the sac as much as possible, moving the point of the syringe in different directions so as to bring the fluid in contact with every portion of the cyst wall. 4. See that no sebaceous matter remains, indicating that a portion, at least, of the cyst retains its vitality.—*Medical and Surgical Reporter.*

Dr. Pepper's Clinic, Hospital of University of Pennsylvania. —Ulcer of the Stomach.—A specimen of the stomach of a man who had just died of severe and repeated hæmatemeis was exhibited to the class, showing two ulcers of considerable size. One of these was found to have perforated the mucous and muscular layer. This complaint is very common in women, especially among the young. The causes are various and well-known. In the instance under consideration the spleen was found to be unusually enlarged—probably the result of a previous attack of malarial fever—its fibrous elements being thickened and the malpighian corpuscles hypertrophied. The ulceration was evidently brought on by the turgescence of the blood-vessels of the stomach produced by the obstruction of the splenic circulation.

The treatment of gastric ulcers is by astringents. Nitrate of silver, in the form of pills, should be given in full doses after meals. Among other remedies, the persalts of iron, the subnitrate of bismuth, and the sulphate of copper are useful. If there be much pain, opium, hydrocyanic acid, chloroform may be administered. An exclusive milk diet is preferable. Beef-juice, gruel, and arrowroot can be taken with safety. All solid food must be avoided. At the time of hemorrhage, absolute rest must be insisted upon; pieces of cracked ice should be swallowed; Monsell's solution, tannic or gallic acid should be given internally; morphia may be given by the mouth and ergotina hypodermically, and all food must be administered by enemata for the time.

Epithelioma of the Neck of the Uterus Cured by Five Injections of a Solution of Chloride of Zinc, by Professor A. Guichard. (Condensed by the Translator).—When an epithelioma of the neck of the uterus is *confined* to that locality, two methods of cure can be employed—amputation and cauterization. The author presented a case in his clinic at the Ecole de Medecine, a woman aged 38 with the following history: She menstruated at 15 years, had two children when respectively 22 and 25 years of age; both now dead; family history good. Present disease began nine months ago, general malaise, etc. Three months ago began to flow at irregular intervals. Speculum neck—examination revealed an epithelioma confined to the posterior dimensions, 5 by 4 centimetre. The tumor bled at the slightest touch. November 30th, assisted by Dr. Guichard, Pere and Briand, the professor injected, with a hypodermic syringe, armed with a long nozzle, 4 drops (or 20 centigrammes) of a solution of chloride of zinc. A tampon was introduced, which was removed the second day and emollient injections made. December 4th, tumor looked shriveled. At three points 5 drops of chloride of zinc were injected. An eschar came away December 6th. As she expected to menstruate by the 11th, no further injections were made. Menstruation lasted from December 12th to 15th. December 18th examination revealed many points that had an appearance of vegetation. At three different points again 5 drops were injected. December 24th and 28th the last injections were made at two points. After this, repeated applications of the solution were made. Two years thereafter, January, 1877, she was examined and found to be well, no return of the disease having taken place.—(*Annales de Gynecologie*.)

Medical Education at Philadelphia.—The University at Philadelphia has at length decided to follow Harvard's example and to adopt the graded coerse. The details will be found in the letter from our Philadelphia correspondent, which we publish to-day. The younger members of the faculty have long advocated the change, but the older ones have opposed it, and it is evident that this step has not been taken without a very limited counting of the cost. The faculty wish to do right, but to do so as cheaply as possible; thus we find that measures have been taken to avoid a very serious diminution of receipts. The plan is by no means so radically changed as it was at Harvard in 1871, for a year includes only five months, and we see that third-year students are to be admitted at half price. We are still ignorant how thorough the examinations are to be at the end of each year, and how strictly proficiency will be demanded before the student is allowed to pass from one class to another. It is on this that it depends whether or not a real advance in medical education will be obtained. We think our Philadelphia friends would have found it better policy, and it certainly would have been more dignified, to have boldly made a radical change and to have trusted to their merits for success. They are, however, entitled to praise for what they have done, and we hope that in a few years the University will stand on a level with Harvard, though the advances constantly made by the latter render this very unlikely, unless the University adopts a more vigorous policy. We hope that in any case, at least, one New York school will feel the necessity of following Boston and Philadelphia.—*Boston Med. and Sur. Journal.*

Local Anesthesias Cured by Metals.—Professor Charcot communicated to the Society of Biology, session January 13, the results of some experiments in the treatment of anæsthetic surfaces by the application of metals, a treatment he had practiced with Dr. Bury at the Saltpetriére. In several hysterical cases the application of 1-2 two franc pieces to anæsthetic surfaces restored sensibility in from fifteen to twenty minutes in a circumference of five, six, eight, or ten ctm., below and above the surface upon which the gold had been laid. The sensibility so restored lasted twenty-four hours. In other hysterical cases, gold is without effect, while copper and zinc are effective. Simultaneously with the return of the sensibility an elevation of temperature is observed, with increase of dynamometric power. Charcot is not willing as yet to venture any explanation. This metallotherapy gives the same results also in anesthesias of cerebral origin.—*The Cincinnati Lancet and Observer.*

An Early Sign of Phthisis.—One of the earliest signs of phthisis to be observed in many cases, before any physical evidence betrays the existence of the disease, is accentuation of the pulmonary tone. This accentuation always betokens, aside from better conduction through more solid lining tissue, a hindrance to the circulation in the pulmonic system. This hindrance in the beginning of the disease depends upon the greater relaxation or lessened elasticity of the lung structure.—*The Cincinnati Lancet and Observer.*

Safe and Rapid Cure for Aneurism.—Dr. Horace Dobell submits to surgeons a simple suggestion for the cure of aneurism. It is to stop the circulation above and below the tumor, remove the fluid contents of the latter by aspiration, and replace them by an injection of spermaceti or stearin. The latter are insoluble in blood, but solid at its temperature; fluid at a temperature low enough to allow of their being safely brought into contact with living tissues, and changes from liquid to solid with great rapidity; and are at the same time light, innocuous and unirritating. Their rapid solidification removes any danger of active or passive clots being washed away when the blood is allowed again to flow, while the time for the operation would be so short that no harm would result to the other tissues on account of the arrested circulation.—*British Medical Journal.*

Treatment of Acute Pneumonia by Turpentine.— Mr. Power, of Dartmoor, observes that oil of turpentine has long been an acknowledged agent of great therapeutic value in acute diseases of the chest. In acute pneumonia he has used it almost to the exclusion of other remedies. For many years he has adopted the following treatment with great success: First, a hot terebinthinate stupe is applied until the skin is well reddened; then a little plain oil of turpentine sprinkled over the affected part; finally, a blanket wrung out of boiling water, covered with a dry blanket. Mr. Power has had patients delirious and gasping for breath, with sordes on the lips (patients who should have seen the doctor twelve hours previously), fall asleep as the last blanket was applied, and awake out of danger. The internal remedies subsequently used were quinine and tincture of perchloride of iron. Diet: milk and water, beef-tea, lemonade, *ad libitum*, occasionally wine. The application of the turpentine to little children must, of course, be modified to suit the age. In all cases he kept on the swathe three or four days or more, uninterruptedly. He has also found that, as a rule, the active treatment need not be pursued very long, the patient being generally out of danger in twenty-four or forty-eight hours. The sequelæ of pneumonia are much modified; frequently altogether escaped. — *The British Medical Journal.*

The Evolution of the Placenta.—A late article by Prof. Turner, in the *Journal of Anatomy and Physiology*, states that in mammalia the same essential constitutents are found entering into the formation of all placentæ, and the simplest arrangement of these may be looked upon as constituting a placenta in its most generalized form. Such a fundamental type of placenta would consist of a fetal portion, composed of a vascular membrane, upon the face one of which is laid down a layer of pavement epithelium, and a maternal portion similar in constitution, with the exception that in this case the epithelium is of the columnar type. These two membranes are applied to each, so that their epithelial surfaces are in contact. From this simple type-form the different varieties of placenta may be conceived to be evolved, the process of evolution being effected by " the assumption of a greater extent of complexity in the foldings, on the one hand of the villous chorion, on the other hand of the uterine mucous membrane with, in in addition, in some placentæ, modifications in the relative size of the maternal blood-vessels, and in the form of the maternal epithelial cells." The diffused placenta presents the closest affinity in structure to the fundamental type, whilst the human placenta is the most specialized. But the author goes on to explain, that whilst this evolution of the more complicated placentæ out of the more simple placentæ is quite conceivable, yet the evolution cannot be regarded as taking place as a continuous process, ".from the diffused to the polycotyledonary, zonary, and dome-shaped group forms, until at length the highly specialized discoid placenta of monkeys and of man has been produced.—*Med. and Sur. Reporter.*

Careless Prescribing.—A physician in New York city lately wrote the following prescription for a lady:

 ℞. Hydrargyri chloridi,   gr. vj
    Pulveris opii,   gr. j.   M.
Sig.—For one dose.

The druggist's clerk put up six grains of corrosive sublimate and one grain of powdered opium. The patient swallowed it, and only by very prompt measures and after great suffering escaped with her life. The physician told a reporter that he had never written otherwise for these drugs, and that the prescription was correct. Such carelessness or ignorance cannot be too severely condemned. The word *mite* or *corrosivum* is directed to be added, to distinguish the mercuric chlorides, and to omit them is unpardonable negligence.—*Med. and Surg. Reporter*.

Treatment of Granular Lids by Acetate of Lead. — Dr. Pierd'houy, as quoted in the *Practitioner*, after having passed in review the very numerous and various methods of treating this disease, expresses himself in favor of Buy's plan, which consists in the application of the neutral acetate of lead in the dry form to the granulations. The acetate should be perfectly fresh, and may be applied lightly with a brush to the granulations after everting the lids; before replacing them the surface should be brushed over with a mixture of oil and glycerine. The reaction is slight, and may be repeated many days consecutively till the granulations are quite flattened down. The plan is well adapted for those who can only be seen occasionally. It has a powerful effect in diminishing the amount of suppuration. It soon produces a cure, and there is no chance of the formation of cicatrices.

Medical Notes.

In Germany, according to the *Medical Times and Gazette*, it has long been the law that druggists shall refuse to dispense a second time any prescriptions which contain "drastic, emetic, diuretic, emmenagogue, narcotic, or other similar powerful medicines," unless the physician who wrote the prescription append the word *reiteratur*. The law has of late fallen into neglect, but a ministerial circular has recently been issued recalling the attention of druggists to it, and requiring its strict observance.

It may be that in this country it would be impolitic to enforce a similar custom by legislation, but could it not be practically accomplished if the pharmaceutical societies were to resolve that their members should not repeat a prescription unless an order were given to that effect by the physician who wrote it? In this way patients would be prevented from indefinitely continuing the use of a medicine which, although at first beneficial, might in time become inactive or harmful, and the common practice of lending prescriptions to friends would be stopped—a custom which often does harm to the sufferer, and is an act of injustice to the physician who is "paid for prescribing for half-a-dozen people only at the rate for which he gives his time and experience to a single individual."

Communications.

SACRAMENTO, June 7, 1877.

R. A. McLEAN, M. D.:

Dear Sir:—At the last meeting of the Sacramento Society for Medical Improvement, held May 23d, the inclosed resolution was adopted and ordered published in the medical journals of the State. I, therefore, send you the resolution, trusting that it will appear in the next number of the *Western Lancet*, as part of the proceedings of our Society.

Respectfully yours,
F. W. HATCH, JR.,
Secretary.

Whereas, an assault was made upon Dr. G. G. Tyrrell, a member of this Society, at the close of the last session of the State Medical Society in San Francisco, by Dr. J. D. Whitney; and whereas the said assault appears to have been uncalled for by any acts done by Dr. Tyrrell on that occasion, except in an official capacity, the said assault being unjustifiable in its conception, and cowardly in its execution; Therefore,

Resolved: That we, the members of the Sacramento Society for Medical Improvement, deprecate the conduct of Dr. J. D. Whitney on the occasion referred to, and sustain Dr. Tyrrell in his action as an officer of the State Society.

Editorial.

In our report of the transactions of the State Medical Society at its last meeting, we inadvertently omitted the names of Drs. W. H. A. Hodgdon and L. M. F. Wanzer in the list of the new members elected.

Errata—In the LANCET for April, a slight typographical error occurred in Dr. Regensburger's article on the treatment of diphtheria, in which, on page 84, thirtieth line from top, the ounce sign was printed when the drachm sign was intended. A marginal correction was made at the time, but it seems that it was not sufficient to prevent a misapprehension of Dr. Regensburger's meaning.

THE Medical Department of the University of Pennsylvania has recently adopted the graded system of medical instruction, somewhat after the mode of Harvard. The Professors all have regular salaries, and students are required to spend three years in attendance upon lectures. Students who are now matriculants are not effected by the change, except at their own request.

The Class of the Medical Department of the University of Cal.—The Summer course of lectures commenced in this institution with a much larger number of students than was anticipated, owing to the general depression in business.

NEARLY every other nation of Europe having led the way, Russia is about adopting the metric weights and measures. The special committee which is sitting at St. Petersburg, at the head-quarters of the Russian Imperial Technical Society, have not only come to the conclusion that such an innovation would be useful, but have also emphatically declared that the present is the fitting moment for the introduction of the metric system. They think that the change ought to be accomplished within two years. It is a remarkable fact that Americans, with all their boasted readiness to adopt labor-saving inventions, and having led the world in use of a decimal currency, should be one of the very last nations of the globe to adopt what John Quincy Adams, in his official report, pronounces the greatest invention of human ingenuity since that of printing, and a greater labor-saver than steam.

Chlorine vs. Carbolic Acid in Surgery.—Dr. A. B. Crosby, in a recent number of the *Archives of Clinical Surgery*, contributes an interesting paper on Cleanliness in Surgery. He is of the opinion that the success of the antiseptic method of Lister depends more upon the scrupulous cleanliness which that method necessitates than upon the antiseptic power of carbolic acid. He urges the rigid observance of every detail conducive to perfect cleanliness. As disinfectants he prefers the chlorinated washes to carbolic acid. He has found carbolic acid much less efficacious than chlorine in checking putrefaction.

Dr. Crosby's experience in the surgical wards of the Bellevue Hospital has been extensive, and his views coincide perfectly with what we have observed in the surgical wards of the City and County Hospital for the last five years. In Professor Toland's wards the saturated solution of chlorate of potassa is used in all cases where antiseptics are indicated. Fetor is prevented, and where present, is promptly destroyed. Suppuration is lessened, and pyemia is unknown. Several outbreaks of erysipelas and gangrene have occurred in the hospital, but in these wards no fatal cases have resulted. In the other surgical wards where carbolic acid is used the epidemics of erysipelas and gangrene have been severer, and in several instances fatal cases have occurred.

It is not alone as an antiseptic wash that chlorate of potassa is useful. Applied as a saturated solution on lint to the stump after amputation, it makes an excellent dressing. It prevents fetor and limits suppuration, while it does not produce a succulent condition of granulating surfaces as the plain water dressing is apt to do. Indeed, it seems to deplete the tissues slightly with which it comes in contact, a property which may be accounted for by the laws of osmosis. It is well known that a solution of pronounced alkalinity will attract to itself, though an animal membrane, fluid alkaline to a less degree. The saturated solution of chlorate of potassa possessing a higher degree of alkalinity than the serum of the blood, and consequently a current is established from the tissues to the dressing.

Book Reviews.

REPORT ON MEDICAL EDUCATION, to THE MEDICAL SOCIETY OF CALIFORNIA, APRIL 18, 1876. By Arthur B. Stout, M. D. Read by Joseph M. Browne, M. D., U. S. N., Chairman of the Standing Committee on Medical Education, as a Supplement to this Report.

Among the many excellent papers read at the late meeting of the State Medical Society none was more attentively listened to than the report by Dr. Stout; an omen, we venture to hope, that some of its recommendations will, at no distant day, be strongly urged by the Society.

The important and yet somewhat hackneyed subject of medical education is discussed in a manner remarkable alike for its terseness and comprehensiveness. A sketch is first given of the gradual development of scientific education from 1840 to the present time. As the demand for more thorough training became general the old system of rostrum lectures was supplemented by hospital training, laboratory work, rehearsals, and surgical operations on the subject. Although the author admits that the majority of American colleges do not fill this programme, yet he is of the opinion that colleges can be so organized as to carry out the most thorough course of training. A charter should be granted only to such corporations as can produce evidence of a paid-up capital, sufficiently large to insure ample salaries to its professors, and to furnish laboratories, etc. "Each professor, in every branch, especially in surgery and anatomy, should be provided with assistants to 'quiz,' and to aid in the actual practice of the *minutiæ* of his department."

"The noble endowment of the United States Government of the University of California places our favored State in the front line of educational improvement. When its comprehensive programme shall come into full operation no further educational charters should be granted. Up to the present time, however, its medical department, after its first inauguration, has been left to sink or swim as it might. But for the munificent donation of Dr. Toland the former alternative might have been its fate. We desire, now, that the treaty stipulations be fulfilled, and that the medical department be allowed all the advantages of its most favored collateral colleges. Hence the claim of the society is justified, that salaried professors should be provided, who shall not be wearied with the toil, nor careworn with the necessity of the practice of medicine, but who shall devote their entire energies to their respective chairs—clinical professors being limited to their hospitals."

In recapitulation, the author suggests the following programme:

"1st. A national institute for the highest stand-point in learning.

"2d. State Universities, not more than two, in each State, for emulation sake—endowed as before proposed.

"3d. Free instruction to the students or aspirants who shall possess the required attainments, showing but limited favor to a poor applicant, to boost him along because he may be poor; nor any concession to the rich, because of their wealth.

"4th. A larger curriculum than is now required," etc.

While there is much that is commendable in the suggestions of Dr. Stout, we are disposed to think too much is aimed at to begin with. It is quite evident that the time has not yet arrived for the carrying out of the system inaugurated by Harvard, and recently adopted by the University of Pennsylvania.

Should such a change be made in the Medical Department of the University it would be found that many students, if not nearly all of them, would go to Chicago, St. Louis, or Cincinnati to graduate.

TRANSACTIONS OF THE AMERICAN GYNÆCOLOGICAL SOCIETY. VOLUME I. FOR THE YEAR 1876. Boston: H. O. Houghton & Co.

It will be remembered by our readers that during the Centennial Exhibition and the visit of many gentlemen of the profession of medicine from every country of Europe and State in the Union, an international convention or congress was held and the opportunity thus afforded utilized by some of the leading Gynæcologists of America to organize the "American Gynæcological Society." The preliminary steps taken to this end and the subsequent transactions of the organization, including many valuable papers read, furnish the material of the volume before us. We hail the advent of the Society with joy, recognizing the need of such an organization for many years past. America to-day stands head and front in Gynæcology, and while Britain, France, Germany, and even Italy has had its Society, America has just awakened to the necessity of organization. The papers contained in the first volume of "Transactions" are from the pen of the ablest representatives of the science, and we recognize in the book an accession to this important, aye! the most important practical branch of the science of medicine long wanted, and one that each year will be looked for and greeted with pleasure by every practitioner in the country. As to the society itself, some criticism may be made as to the peculiarities of its constitution and by-laws. These, however, are of such a nature as will cure themselves in time.

We are glad to see that "Gynæcological Transactions" may be had annually of the publishers at the moderate rate of four dollars, and we opine that few libraries will be without them.

CYCLOPÆDIA OF THE PRACTICE OF MEDICINE. EDITED BY DR. H. VON ZIEMSSEN, PROFESSOR OF CLINICAL MEDICINE IN MUNICH, BAVARIA. VOL. XII. DISEASES OF THE BRAIN AND ITS MEMBRANES. BY PROF. H. NOTHNAGEL OF JENA, PROF. E. HITZIG OF ZÜRICH, PROF. F. OBERNIER OF BONN. PROF. O. HEUBNER OF LEIPZIG, AND PROF. G. HUGUENIN OF ZURICH.

Transalted by Henry R. Swanzy, M. D., of Dublin; Charles Emerson, of Concord; Edward H. Bradford, M. D.; Elbridge G. Cutler, M. D.; Robert T. Edes, M. D.; James J. Putnam, M. D.; Frederic C. Shattuck, M. D.; S. G. Webber, M. D. of Boston, and Louis Velder, M. D., of Elmira. New York: William Wood & Co. San Francisco: A. L. Bancroft & Co.

In the volume before us we see exhibited the same good judgment that has distinguished the editor in each and every book he has produced, *viz:* the selection of young, vigorous intellects as authors—men of mature minds and who have enjoyed facilities for observations, gleaning therefrom facts and deductions practical. "Vol. 12," "Diseases of the Brain and its Membranes," has been contributed to by some of the ablest men of Germany, and the matter furnished is valuable to both the specialist and general practitioner. If it has any fault, or rather, its authors, it is verbosity, which, however, characterizes German authors generally. The book is like the several volumes that have preceded it, issued in good style of paper and typography and fills an important place in the series of the " Cyclopædia."

ATLAS OF SKIN DISEASES. By Louis A. Duhring, M. D., Professor of Skin Diseases in the Hospital of the University of Pennsylvania: Physician to the Dispensary for Skin Diseases. Philadelphia, etc., etc. Part II. Philadelphia: J. B. Lippincott & Co. 1877. San Francisco: A. Roman & Co.

Some months since the first ——— of the "Atlas of Skin Diseases" was issued, and we then took occasion to criticise the work.

The aim of the author is good, viz.: to furnish clinical cases in brief, accompanying each with a life-size portrait. The typography and press work are well done, but the colored drawings, like all *American* efforts in the same direction, are simply abominable, being coarse and unfinished.

Apart from the plates the work is excellent, and will furnish a valuable acquisition to any library.

TRANSACTIONS OF THE NEW YORK PATHOLOGICAL SOCIETY. VOLUME I. John C. Peters, M. D., Editor. New York: William Wood & Co. 1876. San Francisco: A. L. Bancroft & Co.

If the first volume of these transactions be an earnest of what is to follow in subsequent publications, the profession have reason to anticipate much that is of value in the study of pathology. In this volume an interesting historical chapter is first presented, showing that the Society was first organized in June, 1844, by Drs. Goldsmith, J. C. Peters, and L. A. Sayre.

Books Received.

TRANSACTIONS OF THE AMERICAN MEDICAL ASSOCIATION. PRIZE ESSAY: SUPPLEMENT TO VOLUME 27. 1876. Roman & Co.: San Francisco.

HEATON ON RUPTURE. Roman & Co.

Health Reports.

Report of Deaths.

For the Month of May, 1877, in Sacramento City, Cal.

	Sex.		Ages											Nativity.				Race.			Stillborn.
	Male.	Female.	Under 1 year.	1 to 5 years.	5 to 10 years.	10 to 20 years.	20 to 30 years.	30 to 40 years.	40 to 50 years.	50 to 60 years.	60 to 70 years.	70 to 80 years.	80 to 90 years.	90 to 100 years	Unknown.	Pacific States.	Atlantic St's.	Foreign.	Unknown.	White.	Black	Chinese.	
Total.	23	15	9	8	0	2	6	4	6	1	0	2	0	0	0	19	10	9		36	0	2	

Meteorological Record (Means),

For the Month of May, 1877, in Sacramento City, Cal.

Mean Temperature.					Barometer.			Rel. Humidity.			Ins. Rain.
7 A.M.	2 P.M.	9 P.M.	Maxim'm	Minim'm	7 A.M.	2 P.M.	9 P.M.	7 A.M.	2 P.M.	9 P.M.	
57.2	73.8	52.8	77.9	43.7	29.62	29.59	29.56	78	62	73	0.64

F. W. HATCH, M. D.,
Secretary Board of Health

Health Reports.

Abstract of the Reports of Deaths and their Causes in the following Cities and Towns of California during February, 1877.

CITIES AND TOWNS.	Total Deaths.	PREVALENT DISEASES.										AUTHORITIES.
		Consumption.	Pneumonia.	Bronchitis.	Other Dis. of the Lungs.	Diarrhœa & Dysentery.	Other Dis. Stom. & Bow.	Diphtheria.	Scarlatina.	Measles.	Typho-Malarial Fevers.	
San Francisco	497	45	23	5	9	1	12	122	5	1	8	S. F. Board of Health
Sacramento	19	5	1	0	1	0	0	1	0	0	0	Sac. " "
Stockton	10	4	0	0	0	0	0	4	0	0	1	Stockton "
Petaluma	5	0	0	0	0	0	0	2	0	0	1	Dr. J. H. Crane.
Dixon	1	1	0	0	0	0	0	0	0	0	0	Dr. A. H. Pratt.
Los Angeles	a71	4	0	0	0	0	3	8	0	1	3	Dr. H. S. Orme.
Truckee	3	0	1	0	0	0	0	0	0	0	0	Dr. W. Curless.
St. Helena and vic.	1	0	0	0	0	0	0	0	0	0	0	Dr. C. F. A. Michell
Napa City	0	0	0	0	0	0	0	0	0	0	0	
Watsonville	2	1	0	0	0	0	0	0	0	0	0	Dr. W. D. Rodgers.
Folsom	1	1	0	0	0	0	0	0	0	0	0	Dr. F. C. Durant.
Santa Cruz	12	0	0	0	0	0	0	8	0	0	0	Dr. C. L. Anderson.
Suisun & Fairfield	0	0	0	0	0	0	0	0	0	0	0	
Colusa	0	0	0	0	0	0	0	0	0	0	0	
Santa Barbara	21	4	0	0	0	0	1	10	0	0	0	Dr. C. B. Bates.
Tulare Co. Visalia & vic	0	0	0	0	0	0	0	0	0	0	0	
Yreka, Siskiyou Co.	4	0	3	0	0	0	0	0	1	0	0	Dr. Daniel Ream.
Downieville & vicin.	4	0	1	0	0	0	0	0	2	0	0	Dr. Alemby Jump.
Antioch	3	0	0	0	0	0	2	0	0	0	0	Dr. M. C. Parkison.
Woodbridge & vicinity	0	0	0	0	0	0	0	0	0	0	0	
Cloverdale	2	0	0	0	0	0	0	1	0	0	0	Dr. Q. C. Smith.
Woodland	3	3	0	0	0	0	0	0	0	0	0	Dr. Thos. Ross.
Adin, Modoc Co.	0	0	0	0	0	0	0	0	0	0	0	
Cedarville, Modoc	1	0	0	0	0	0	0	0	0	0	0	Dr. W. H. Patterson
Modesto, Stanislaus	6	1	0	0	0	0	0	4	0	0	0	Dr. Jos. A. Jackson.
San Jose and Santa Clara	0	0	0	0	0	0	0	0	0	0	0	
Millville, Shasta Co.	0	0	0	0	0	0	0	0	0	0	0	Dr. F. R. Brown.
Weaverville, Trinity Co	0	0	0	0	0	0	0	0	0	0	0	
Lakeport	2	0	0	0	0	0	0	0	0	0	0	Dr. H. J. Crumpton
Winters, Yolo Co.	0	0	0	0	0	0	0	0	0	0	0	Dr. W. T. Bell.
Ventura	4	0	1	0	0	0	1	1	0	0	0	Dr. F. Delmont.
Willows, Colusa Co.	7	0	0	0	0	0	0	0	0	0	2	Dr. W. C. Baylor.
San Mateo Co. Redwood	11	3	1	0	0	b1	1	1	0	0	1	Dr. O. A. Kirkpatrick.
Davisville	3	0	1	0	1	0	0	0	0	0	0	Dr. M. Gardner.
Total deaths	693	72	32	5	11	2	20	162	8	2	16	

NOTE.—a. 43 of these by Small Pox.
b. 1 Cholera Infantum.

Report of Deaths Registered in San Francisco During the Month of May, 1877.

Diseases.	Total.	Per Cent.	Under 5 Years	5 to 20 Years.	From 20 to 50 Years	From 50 to 70 Years.	Over 70 Years.	Unknown.	Male.	Female.	California.	Other Parts of U. S.	China.	Other Countries.	Unknown
1—Small Pox	6				6				4	2		2	2	2	
Measles															
Scarlatina															
Diphtheria	62		42	19	1				31	31	52	8		2	
Croup	8		4	4					6	2	7			1	
Whooping Cough	4		4						4		3			1	
Typhus and Typhoid Fevers	15		2	5	7	1			7	8	15	4	6	5	
Diarrhœa and Dysentery	3		3							3	3				
Cholera Infantum	5		5						2	3	5				
Cholera Morbus															
Pyemia and Septicemia	1			1						1	1				
Cerebro-Spinal Meningitis	2		1	1					2		2				
Syphilis															
Alcoholism	2				2				2					2	
2—Cancer	11				7	2	2		8	3		4		7	
Phthisis Pulmonalis	58		1	3	44	10			36	22	7	14	3	34	
Hydrocephalus & Tubercular Meningitis	3		1	2						3	3				
3—Encephalitis	13		9	1	2	1			9	4	8			5	
Apoplexy and Paralysis	17			1	9	7			11	6	1	2		13	1
Convulsions	14		14						8	6	14				
Other Diseases of the Nervous System	7		3		3	1			4	3	3	2		2	
Aneurism	5				4	1			4	1		2		3	
Diseases of the Heart	18			1	8	7	2		9	9		6		12	
Pneumonia	23		2		9	11	1		17	6	2	2		17	2
Bronchitis	3				1	2			2	1		1		2	
Other Diseases of the Respiratory Organs	8		2		3	2	1		5	3	2	1		5	
Diseases of the Stomach and Bowels	19		8		9	2			12	7	8			11	
Diseases of the Liver	3				1	2			3			1		2	
Bright's Disease and Nephritis	3				3				2	1		1		2	
4—Puerperal Diseases	5				5					5	1			4	
5 Atrophy, Inanition and Old Age	44		27	1	2	4	10		25	19	27	4		13	
—Suicides	4				3	1			3	1		1		3	
Deaths in Institutions	93		16	2	51	23	2		73	20	18	12	2	59	2
Still-Births									11	19					
										30					
1 - Zymotic Diseases	113	25.4	63	31	17	2			61	52	81	16	2	14	
2—Constitutional Diseases	73	16.4	2	5	52	12	2		45	28	10	18	3	42	
3—Local Diseases	146	32.9	43	4	56	38	5		96	50	43	21	1	78	3
4—Developmental Diseases	56	12.6	33	1	8	4	10		29	27	34	4		18	
5—Deaths from Violence	15	3.4	3	2	9	1			12	3	3	5	1	6	
Deaths from Unknown Causes { Chinese	34	7.9	1		31	2			28	6	1		33		
Deaths from Unknown Causes { Others	7	1.4	3		2	2			3	4	3	1		3	
Total	444		148	43	175	61	17		274	170	175	65	40	161	3
Per Cent. to Total Mortality		100.0	33.3	9.7	39.4	13.9	3.7		61.7	38.3	39.4	14.6	9.1	36.7	0.2

Estimated population March, 1877..300,000

J. L. MEARES, M. D.,
Health Officer.

MEDICAL BOOKS.

We call the attention of MEDICAL STUDENTS to the following list of TEXT BOOKS adopted by the CALIFORNIA MEDICAL COLLEGES:

Book	Size	Binding	Cloth	Sheep
FLINT'S Practice of Medicine	8vo	Cloth	$6 00	Sheep $7 00
AITKEN'S " "	"	"	12 00	" 14 00
GRAY'S Anatomy	"	"	6 00	" 7 00
WILSON'S "	"	"	4 00	" 5 00
WOOD'S U. S. Dispensatory, 14th Ed.	"			" 10 00
TANNER'S Clinical Medicine	12mo	"	1 50	"
DA COSTA'S " "	8vo	"	6 00	" 7 00
BEDFORD'S Obstetrics	"	"	5 50	" 6 50
BIDDLE'S Materia Medica	"	"	4 00	" 5 00
DALTON'S Physiology	"	"	5 50	" 6 50
FLINT'S "	"	"	6 00	" 7 00
HOLMES Surgery	"	"	6 00	" 7 00
GROSS' " [2 vols]				" 15 00
ERICHSEN'S "	"	"	9 00	" 11 00
DUNGLISON'S Medical Dictionary	"	"	6 50	" 7 50
HAMILTON on Fractures	"	"	5 75	" 6 75
TAYLOR'S Medical Jurisprudence	"	"	5 00	" 6 00
FOWNE'S Chemistry	12mo	"	2 75	" 3 25
BARKER'S "	"	"	1 75	
STELLWAG On the Eye	8vo	"	7 00	" 8 00
WELL'S " "	8vo	"	5 00	" 6 00
TROELSCH On the Ear	"	"	4 50	" 5 50
THOMAS On Diseases of Women	"	"	5 00	" 6 00
MEIGS & PEPPER On Diseases of Children	"	"	6 00	" 7 00
MAUDSLEY'S Physiology and Pathology of the Mind	8vo	Cloth		3 00
BUMSTEAD On Venereal	8vo	Cloth	5 00	Sheep 6 00
WOOD'S Materia Medica	"	"	5 50	" 6 50
WILSON On Skin Disease, (Plates)	"	"		10 00
TAYLOR On Poisons	"	"	5 50	" 6 50
LOOMIS' Physical Diagnosis	"	"		3 00
LEISHMAN'S Midwifery	"	"	5 00	" 6 00
BILLROTH'S Surgical Pathology	"	"	5 00	" 6 00

A FULL LINE OF STANDARD MEDICAL BOOKS ALWAYS IN STOCK.

NEW BOOKS received constantly.

A liberal discount allowed students and the "Profession."

A. ROMAN & CO.

Booksellers and Stationers,

No. 11 Montgomery Street,

Lick House Block,   San Francisco.

University of California,

MEDICAL AND SURGICAL DEPARTMENT.

Circular of the Medical College,

Toland Hall, San Francisco, Session 1877.

Board of Regents:

His Excellency WM. IRWIN, Governor, *ex-officio* President of the Board.
His Honor J. A. JOHNSON, Lieutenant-Governor.
Hon. G. D. CARPENTER, Speaker of the Assembly.
Hon. EZRA S. CARR, State Superintendent of Public Instruction.
R. S. CAREY, Esq., President of the State Agricultural Society.
A. S. HALLIDIE, Esq., President of the Mechanics' Institute of San Francisco.
JOHN LECONTE, M. D., Oakland, President of the University.

Jos. W. WINANS, Esq., San Francisco.	Hon. JOHN S. HAGER, San Francisco.
J. MORA MOSS, Esq., Oakland.	A. J. BOWIE, M. D., San Francisco.
Rev. H. STEBBINS, D. D., San Francisco.	D. O. MILLS, Esq., S. F., Treasurer.
Hon. LAWRENCE ARCHER, San Jose.	Hon. JOHN B. FELTON, Oakland.
J. WEST MARTIN, Esq., Oakland.	F. M. PIXLEY, Esq., San Francisco.
Hon. SAMUEL B. McKEE, Oakland.	Hon. EUGENE CASSERLY, San Francisco.
WILLIAM MEEK, Esq., San Lorenzo.	W. T. WALLACE.
JOHN F. SWIFT, Esq., San Francisco.	
J. M. HAMILTON, Esq., Guenoc.	

The President of the University is present at the meeting of the Board and is a member of the Standing Committee.

Secretary,
ROBERT E. C. STEARNS, Berkeley.

Advisory Committee,
MESSRS. HAIGHT, MARTIN AND STEBBINS.

Active Members of the Faculty:

JOHN LECONTE, M. D., President.

H. H. TOLAND, M. D.,
   Professor of Principles of Surgery and Clinical Surgery.
R. BEVERLY COLE, M. D.,
   Professor of Obstetrics and Diseases of Women and Children.
A. A. O'NEIL, A. M., M. D.,
   Professor of Anatomy.
C. M. BATES, M. D.,
   Professor of Clinical Medicine.
M. W. FISH, M. D.,
   Professor of Physiology.
W. T. BRADBURY, M. D.,
   Professor of Materia Medica and Therapeutics.

F. W. HATCH, M. D.,
   Professor of Principles and Practice of Medicine.
G. B. KEENE, M. D.
   Professor of Chemistry.
N. J. MARTINACHE, M. D.,
   Professor of Ophthalmology and Otology.
G. A. SHURTLEFF, M. D.,
   Professor of Mental Diseases.
E. D. MARTINEAUT, M. D.,
   Demonstrator of Anatomy.

The regular Annual Course of Lectures in this Institution will commence on the first Monday in June and terminate on the thirty-first day of October, 1877.

A. A. O'NEIL, M. D., Dean of the Faculty,
Office, 650 Washington Street.

---

* NOTE.—A Dental College and a Pharmaceutical College have been established in connection with the Medical and Surgical Department of the University of California.

TOLAND HALL, cor. Stockton and Chestnut Sts.

DR. GARRATT'S ELECTRIC DISK,

 for local Weakness and chronic Pains—if worn by night, or day, as a flexible pad, self-applies a constant fine Electric *influence*, of great power to cure weak Nerves, Joints, Muscles or Organs, as weak Lungs, Throat, Stomach or Back, Sluggish Liver, Rheumatic Heart, Asthma, Congestion in Neck, Head Pains, Weak Kidneys and Pelvic organs.

Large best Disk, 5 by 8 inches, 24 poles, $2.50. Children's, 2 by 5, $1. Simple Disk, 50 cents. Greatly improved in durability. Each Disk is *warranted*.

Physicians say, "Garratt's Disk is the only thing *for this purpose* that is reliable."

Sold by Druggists and Surgical Instrument Dealers.

Sent by mail on receipt of price, by A. C. GARRATT, M. D. (Electrician), 6 Hamilton Place, Boston, Mass.

The New York Medical Journal.

Edited by JAMES B. HUNTER, M. D.,

Assistant Surgeon to the New York State Woman's Hospital; Consulting Surgeon to the New York Infirmary for Women and Children; Member of the New York Obstetrical Society.

The leading features of this Journal are the following:

ORIGINAL COMMUNICATIONS FROM EMINENT MEMBERS OF THE PROFESSION.

REPORTS OF INTERESTING CASES IN PRIVATE PRACTICE.

NOTES OF PRACTICE IN METROPOLITAN HOSPITALS, ILLUSTRATING THE USE OF NEW METHODS AND NEW REMEDIES.

TRANSLATIONS AND EXTRACTS GIVING THE CREAM OF ALL THE FOREIGN JOURNALS.

REPORTS ON MEDICINE, SURGERY, OBSTETRICS, GYNÆCOLOGY, LARYNGOLOGY, PATHOLOGY, ETC.

CRITICAL AND IMPARTIAL REVIEWS OF ALL NEW MEDICAL BOOKS.

PROCEEDINGS OF MEDICAL SOCIETIES.

COPIOUS ILLUSTRATION BY MEANS OF WOODCUTS.

THE LATEST GENERAL MEDICAL INTELLIGENCE.

A General Index to the NEW YORK MEDICAL JOURNAL, from its first issue to June, 1876—including twenty-three volumes—now ready.

A new volume of the NEW YORK MEDICAL JOURNAL begins with the numbers for January and July each year. Subscriptions received for any period.

Terms: $4 per Annum. Postage prepaid by the Publishers.

Remittances, invariably in advance, should be made to

D. APPLETON & CO., Publishers, 549 and 551 Broadway, N. Y.

BURRINGTON'S
DR. WADSWORTH'S
UTERINE ELEVATOR.

The most simple and practical of any ever invented. It is made of India-rubber, *without lead*, unirritating, of easy application, and unfailingly keeps the womb in its natural position. The first-class physicians in Providence, and eminent practitioners in almost every State, highly recommend it. A pamphlet describing it, and testimonials of distinguished physicians, also price list, sent on application.

H. H. BURRINGTON,
Sole Proprietor, Providence, R. I.

Also for sale by J. H. A. FOLKERS & BRO., San Francisco, Cal., and by dealers in Surgical Instruments generally.

The Cream of Medical Literature.

THIRTY-FIFTH YEAR OF REPUBLICATION.

BRAITHWAITE'S RETROSPECT:

A Half-Yearly Journal of Practical Medicine and Surgery,

Containing a retrospective view of every Discovery and Practical Improvement in the Medical Sciences, digested from the leading Medical Journals of Europe and America.

Republished every January and July since 1840.

This invaluable compendium, which was commenced in 1840, is issued simultaneously with the London edition, by virtue of an arrangement entered into with its distinguished editor, and appears regularly in *January* and *July* of each year.

The peculiar excellence of the "RETROSPECT" consists in the fact that it embodies in a confined space, after careful perusal, all the cream of all the Medical periodicals—preserving all the essentially practical articles of discovery and improvement. The great advantage offered to practitioners by this method is the saving them time, labor, and money. It constitutes a

CONDENSED REGISTER OF MEDICAL FACTS

and observations for the past year, and presents a complete retrospect of all that is valuable and worth possessing, gleaned from the current Medical Literature of the time.

This admirable *digest* enjoys, throughout the world, a higher fame in its department, and has a more extensive patronage, than any other Medical Journal extant. The terms offered are more liberal than those of any other periodical, as will be seen below. The subscription price is only $2.50 to regular annual subscribers, who invariably pay in *advance of publication*; all Parts after publication, one or more, $1.50 each.

☞ On the receipt of **$4**, BRAITHWAITE and PHYSICIAN's MONITOR, one year, and the PHYSICIAN's HAND-BOOK, revised, for 1876, *free of postage.*

☞ On the receipt of **$10**, *accompanied with names of five* NEW *subscribers, the* "RETROSPECT" *will be mailed to each subscriber's address, one year, free of postage.*

Communications should be addressed to

W. A. TOWNSEND, Publisher,

P. O. Box 5108.   177 Broadway, New York.

NINETEENTH YEAR OF PUBLICATION OF

THE PHYSICIAN'S HAND-BOOK,

NEW IMPROVED EDITION FOR 1876, CONTAINING ALL THE NEW REMEDIAL AGENTS. BY WILLIAM ELMER, M. D.

NOW PUBLISHED Bound in English Morocco, Red Edges, Pocket-book form. Price Reduced to $1.75 with printed matter, and $1.50 printed matter omitted.

THE PHYSICIAN'S HAND-BOOK now enters its *NINETEENTH YEAR* of publication. This popular standard Manual has received the most flattering encomiums from the leading Medical Journals of America and Europe. During the fifth of a century it has become an indispensable companion to every member of the profession who has availed himself of its superior advantages. Improvements have been constantly introduced until it is conceded to be the most perfect work of its class, and the demand for it has steadily increased.

FOR SALE BY ALL BOOKSELLERS AND NEWS DEALERS.

P. O. Box 5108.   Published by W. A. TOWNSEND, 177 Broadway, N. Y.

AGENCY FOR THE

Purchase of Medical Books, also for Subscriptions at Commutation Rates.

ESTABLISHED 1843.

The undersigned has connected with his Publishing business a Department for supplying Medical and Scientific BOOKS AND PERIODICALS FOR PRIVATE INDIVIDUALS, ASSOCIATIONS, LIBRARIES, etc., and for thirty years has made this branch of it a specialty.

He is prepared to supply orders by mail or express, at the LOWEST POSSIBLE PRICES, or all works and periodicals in every department of Medicine and Surgery. The publications of all the leading houses will be furnished on the MOST LIBERAL TERMS offered by the respective publishers. On all annual subscription postage *prepaid* by him, and publishers' *club rates* allowed.

Catalogues supplied free of expense, and estimates given for any number of volumes or sets of works for libraries.

All orders for Books, accompanied by the money at Catalogue prices, will be forwarded to the purchaser, *free of expense*. He will give orders his personal supervision and exercise the utmost care in their prompt execution.

SPECIAL INDUCEMENTS.—On receipt of an order for books, amounting to $15 at publishers' retail prices, a deduction of 10 per cent. will be made; on $25, 12 per cent.; on $50, 15 per cent.; on $100, 20 per cent., exclusive of express charges.

Remittances may be made at his risk, if forwarded by Post-Office Order, Bank Draft Registered Letter.

P. O. Box 5108.   W. A. TOWNSEND, Publisher, 177 Broadway, N. Y.

G. G. BURNETT,
APOTHECARY,
DEALER IN
PURE DRUGS AND MEDICINES,
Fine Perfumery and Toilet Articles,
327 MONTGOMERY STREET,
BETWEEN CALIFORNIA AND PINE,

Under Odd Fellows' Hall,   SAN FRANCISCO.

California State Woman's Hospital,
Corner Howard and Twelfth Streets, San Francisco.

Organized, 1868, — — **Incorporated, 1873.**

SURGEON-IN-CHARGE,	JOHN SCOTT, M. D., F. R. C. S. I.
HOUSE PHYSICIAN,	DR. G. CHISMORE.
ASSISTANT SURGEON,	DR. CHAS. E. BLAKE

Board of Consulting Physicians and Surgeons,

R. BEVERLY COLE, M.D., M. R. C. S., ENG., Special Consultant.

DR. C. McCORMICK,	DR. C. C. KEENY,
DR. C. B. BRIGHAM,	DR. O. O. BURGESS,
DR. J. C. SHORB,	A. J. BOWIE.

This hospital is specially devoted to the treatment of diseases peculiar to women. The Surgeon-in-charge receives no remuneration for his services. Six beds are set apart for free patients; other patients are required to pay a weekly board, as arranged by the Lady Managers. For admission apply to the matron of the hospital, or to

Dr. SCOTT, 607 Folsom Street.

H. PLANTEN & SON,

Established in 1836.   224 WILLIAM ST., N.Y.

CAPSULES!

Pure Copaiba, Copaiba and Cubebs, Cod Liver Oil, Castor Oil, Sandalwood Oil, pure and with 1-10 Cassia, Xylol, Phosphorated Oil, Eucalyptus Globulus, Matico, Apiol,

And many other kinds to which new articles are continually added.

EMPTY CAPSULES (5 SIZES), especially adapted and recommended for the easy administration of concentrated or nauseous solid medical substances, as Powders and Pills.

DETAILED LISTS AND SAMPLES FURNISHED ON APPLICATION.

IMPORTERS OF

NORWAY COD LIVER OIL.

Sole Agents in America for BLAIR'S GOUT AND RHEUMATIC PILLS.

TO THE
Medical Profession and Druggists!

The undersigned has on hand and is now prepared to supply THE PROFESSION and DRUGGISTS with

PURE WHISKEY,

Free from Fusel Oil, Ether, or any Deleterious Substance.

Made by a NEW PROCESS, by means of which the WHISKEY IS ABSOLUTELY PURE.

Manufactured at the WEST END DISTILLERY, SAN FRANCISCO. For sale by

J. B. Snyder,
SOLE AGENT,
No. 226 California Street.

[UNIVERSITY OF CALIFORNIA.]

I have analyzed the Whiskey above named, manufactured at the West End Distillery, and find it to be free from Fusel Oil and other deleterious substances.

OAKLAND, August 1st, 1874.

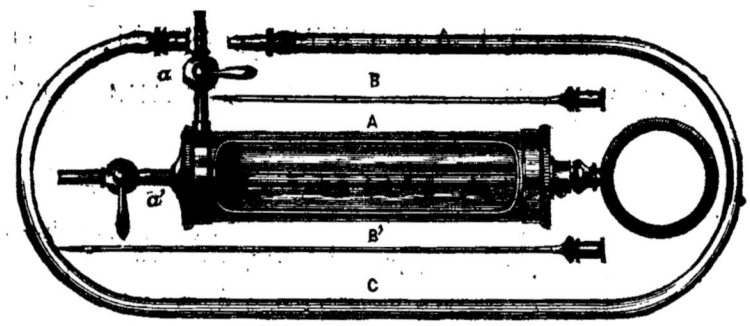

DIEULAFOG'S SMALL ASPIRATOR.

OTTO & REYNDERS,
64 Chatham Street,
NEW YORK.

MANUFACTURERS AND IMPORTERS OF

SURGICAL AND ORTHOPŒDICAL INSTRUMENTS, SKELETONS AND ANATOMICAL PREPARATIONS.

Sole Agents for Seiter's New Hypodermic Syringe.

Aspirators, E. Holden's Sphygmograph, a complete assortment of Aural, Ocular, Laryngeal, Urethral, Uterine, Obstetric, Post Mortem, Minor and General Operating Instruments, Trusses, Abdominal Supporters, Elastic Stockings, etc., etc.

The latest IMPROVEMENTS and NEW INVENTIONS on hand and received constantly from our Agents in Europe.

DR. MARSH'S
Radical Cure Truss,
ALSO
IMPERVIOUS TRUSSES OF VARIOUS FORMS,
For the Permanent Relief of Hernia.

ELASTIC STOCKINGS, SHOULDER BRACES, Supporters, Crutches,

Apparatus for Bow Legs, Club Feet, Weak Ankles, Hip Disease, and all other Physical Deformities, made and accurately fitted at the Radical Cure Truss Office of the

MARSH TRUSS CO.,
513 MONTGOMERY,
Cor. Commercial,   SAN FRANCISCO.

☞ Reference, by permission, to Prof. WILLARD PARKER, Drs. SAYRE, SANDS, CRANE and other eminent Surgeons of this city.

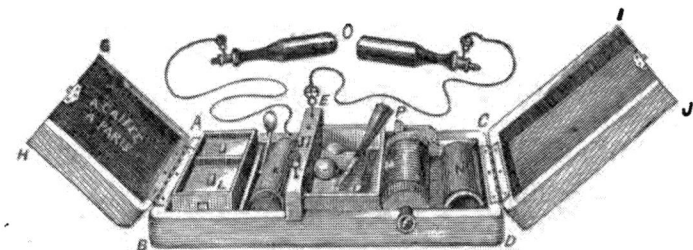

WM. HATTEROTH,

Importer and Manufacturer of

Surgical, Dental and Electrical Instruments.

Sole Agent for D. W. KOLB, Philadelphia.

Apparatus for Deformities, Trusses, Crutches, etc., always on hand or made to order

AT

28 Geary Street,   **Near Kearny,**

SAN FRANCISCO.

Attention of the Profession is respectfully called to my assortment of Electro-Medical apparatus, and the repairing and manufacturing of Instruments, at most reasonable prices and in the best manner. Every article warranted.

☞ Professor R. Beverly Cole's Obstetrical Forceps constantly on hand.

INTERNATIONAL EXHIBITION, PHILADELPHIA, 1876.

AWARD

For "General Excellence in Manufacture."

H. PLANTEN & SON,

Established 1836,   224 William Street, New York.

GELATINE CAPSULES

OF ALL KINDS. ALSO,

Empty Capsules (5 sizes) for the easy administration of nauseous medicinal preparations.

☞ SOLE AGENTS FOR BLAIR'S GOUT AND RHEUMATIC PILLS. ☜

List and Samples sent on application.   SOLD BY ALL DRUGGISTS.

EXTRACT OF MALT

"WITH COD LIVER OIL."

THE MOST DESIRABLE EMULSION OF COD LIVER OIL.

IMPROVED TROMMER'S EXTRACT OF MALT, "WITH COD LIVER OIL," is confidently presented to the medical profession as an *efficient, palatable and perfectly stable combination, consisting of equal parts of the Extract of Canada Barley Malt and the best quality of fresh Cod Liver Oil, flavored with Oil of Bitter Almonds.*

Owing to its disagreeable flavor and liability to disturb the stomach, Physicians are commonly restricted to prescribing Cod Liver Oil for those cases in which it is almost the only resource. It is well known to be equally efficacious in various forms of disease depending upon mal-nutrition. It is believed that the combination of EXTRACT OF MALT with COD LIVER OIL supplies a general and long-felt want, by enabling physicians to extend the use of the oil to all cases in which it is indicated, combined with a substance that increases its efficacy, by making it easily digestible, and acceptable to the most delicate stomach.

Unlike any of the various bulky emulsions proposed with the object of masking the peculiar flavor of the oil, in this combination are found *but two substances*, and these of almost *equal value in the treatment of the same class of diseases.*

The properties possessed by EXTRACT OF MALT of transforming unassimilable food into that which may be easily assimilated, of furnishing phosphates to the system, of being itself exceedingly bland and nutritious, and of forming also *an unequaled emulsion with Cod Liver Oil,* sufficiently attest the appropriateness of the combination.

Each bottle contains sixteen fluid ounces. Price, $1.00.

IMPROVED TROMMER'S EXTRACT OF MALT, "WITH COD LIVER OIL AND IODIDE OF IRON." Iodide of Iron is tonic, alterative, diuretic and emmenagogue, and is often indicated in conjunction with nutrient restoratives. It is chiefly employed in scrofulous complaints, enlarged glands, anæmia, chlorosis, atonic amenorrhœa, leucorrhœa and diabetes. In secondary syphilis occurring in debilitated and scrofulous subjects, Ricord found it a most valuable remedy.

Each dose contains one grain of Iodide of Iron. Price $1.00.

EXTRACT OF MALT

"WITH PEPSIN."

IMPROVED TROMMER'S EXTRACT OF MALT "WITH PEPSIN" is invaluable in *dyspeptic disorders*, and specially adapted to cases characterized by *irritability of the stomach*, or by *nausea*. It is also employed with great advantage in the *wasting diseases of children* both as a nutritive and to improve digestion and assimilation.

This combination, *serving both as food and medicine*, is growing in favor with the profession as a remedy meeting important indications in the *treatment of protracted fevers*, and especially *typhoid fever*, where the prime objects are to support the system and invigorate the enfeebled digestive and assimilative processes.

No article of the Materia Medica approaches EXTRACT OF MALT, "with PEPSIN," as a bland and nutritive substance, *containing all the elements which are required to nourish the body, as well as those (Pepsin Diastase and Hydrochloric Acid) concerned in the digestion of the food proper.* Prof. W. H. Thomson, in his lectures, has well said that "starvation is the second great complication of typhoid fever. After the first violence of the disease has passed and nourishment of the patient becomes all-important, this preparation may be given in teaspoonful doses repeated every two or three hours, with the effect of improving the appetite, increasing the strength and relieving the gastric and intestinal catarrh, and the accompanying diarrhœa and tympanites.

Each tablespoonful dose of the IMPROVED TROMMER'S EXTRACT OF MALT, " with PEPSIN,"
contains of   Pepsin Porci, - - - - 6¼ grains.
                Acid Hydrochloric, - - - 2½ minims.

Each bottle contains sixteen fluid ounces. Price, $1.50.

PREPARED BY:

TROMMER EXTRACT OF MALT CO.,   -   FREMONT, O.

Manufacturers also of the following preparations:

Improved Trommer's Extract of Malt "with Hops."
"   "   "   " "Ferrated."
"   "   "   " "with Hypophosphites."
"   "   "   " "with Iodides."
"   "   "   " "with Alteratives."
"   "   "   " "Cit. Iron and Quinine."

Bellevue Hospital Medical College,
CITY OF NEW YORK.
SESSIONS OF 1877-78.

THE COLLEGIATE YEAR in this Institution embraces a preliminary Autumnal Term the Regular Winter Session, and a Spring Session

THE PRELIMINARY AUTUMNAL TERM for 1877-1878 will open on Wednesday, September 19, 1877, and continue until the opening of the Regular Session. During this term, instruction, consisting of didactic lectures on special subjects and daily clinical lectures will be given, as heretofore, by the entire Faculty. Students expecting to attend the Regular Session are strongly recommended to attend the Preliminary Term, but attendance during the latter is not required. *During the Preliminary Term, clinical and didactic lectures will be given in precisely the same number and order as in the Regular Session.*

THE REGULAR SESSION will begin on Wednesday, October 3, 1877, and end about the 1st of March, 1878.

FACULTY.

ISAAC E. TAYLOR, M. D.,
Emeritus Professor of Obstetrics and Diseases of Women, and President of the Faculty.

JAMES R. WOOD, M. D., LL. D.,
Emeritus Professor of Surgery.

FORDYCE BARKER, M. D.,
Professor of Clinical Midwifery and Diseases of Women.

AUSTIN FLINT, M. D.,
Professor of the Principles and Practice of Medicine and Clinical Medicine.

W. H. VAN BUREN, M. D.,
Professor of Principles and Practice of Surgery, Diseases of Genito-Urinary System, and Clinical Surgery.

LEWIS A. SAYRE, M. D.,
Professor of Orthopedic Surgery, Fractures and Dislocations, and Clinical Surgery.

ALEXANDER B. MOTT, M. D.,
Professor of Clinical and Operative Surgery.

WILLIAM T. LUSK, M. D.,
Professor of Obstetrics and Diseases of Women and Children, and Clinical Midwifery.

EDMUND R. PEASLEE, M.D., LL. D.,
Professor of Gynæcology.

WILLIAM M. POLK, M. D.,
Professor of Materia Medica and Therapeutics, and Clinical Medicine.

AUSTIN FLINT, JR., M. D.,
Professor of Physiology and Physiological Anatomy, and Secretary of the Faculty.

ALPHEUS B. CROSBY, M. D.,
Professor of General, Descriptive, and Surgical Anatomy.

R. OGDEN DOREMUS, M. D., LL. D.
Professor of Chemistry and Toxicology.

EDWARD G. JANEWAY, M. D.,
Professor of Pathological Anatomy Histology, Diseases of the Nervous System, and Clinical Medicine.

PROFESSORS OF SPECIAL DEPARTMENTS, ETC.

HENRY D. NOYES, M. D.,
Professor of Ophthalmology and Otology.

JOHN P. GRAY, M. D., LL. D.,
Professor of Physiological Medicine and Medical Jurisprudence.

EDWARD L. KEYES, M. D.,
Professor of Dermatology, and Adjunct to the Chair of Principles of Surgery.

EDWARD G. JANEWAY, M. D.,
Professor of Practical Anatomy. (Demonstrator of Anatomy.)

LEROY MILTON YALE, M. D.,
Lecturer Adjunct upon Orthopedic Surgery.

A. A. SMITH, M. D.,
Lecturer Adjunct upon Clinical Medicine.

A distinctive feature of the method of instruction in this College is the union of clinical and didactic teaching. All the lectures are given within the Hospital grounds During the Regular Winter Session, in addition to four didactic lectures on every week-day except Saturday, two or three hours are daily allotted to clinical instruction.

The Spring Session consists chiefly of Recitations from Text-books. This term continues from the first of March to the first of June. During this Session, daily recitations in all the departments are held by a corps of examiners appointed by the regular Faculty. Regular clinics are also given in the Hospital and in the College building.

FEES FOR THE REGULAR SESSION.

Fees for Tickets to all the Lectures during the Preliminary and Regular Term,
including Clinical Lectures...$140 00
Matriculation Fee... 5 00
Demonstrator's Ticket (including material for dissection)................... 10 00
Graduation Fee.. 30 00

FEES FOR THE SPRING SESSION.

Matriculation (Ticket good for the following Winter)........................ $5 00
Recitations, Clinics and Lectures... 35 00
Dissection (Ticket good for the following Winter)........................... 10 00

Students who have attended two full Winter courses of Lectures may be examined at the end of their second course upon Materia Medica, Physiology, Anatomy, and Chemistry, and, if successful, they will be examined at the end of their third course upon Practice of Medicine, Surgery, and Obstetrics only.

For the Annual Circular and catalogue, giving regulations for graduation and other information, address Prof. AUSTIN FLINT, JR., Secretary, Bellevue Hospital Medical College.

PROFESSIONAL CARDS, BILLS, PRESCRIPTION BLANKS, ETC., ETC., neatly printed, at very moderate prices.

SPECIAL FACILITIES FOR DRUGGISTS' LABELS, ETC.

Orders sent by mail to P. O. Box 1589, or by Express to 414 Market Street, will receive prompt and careful attention.

MEDICAL BOOKS JUST PUBLISHED.

THE MEDICAL REGISTER AND DIRECTORY OF THE UNITED STATES.

By Samuel W. Butler, M.D. Second Edition, thoroughly revised and enlarged. One Vol., 8vo., 900 pages. Price, prepaid to any address, cloth $5.50; leather $6.50.

This work is of the greatest value to Physicians, Medical Colleges, Life Insurance Companies, Wholesale Druggists, Dealers in Surgical and Medical Supplies, etc. It contains the names and addresses of nearly SEVENTY THOUSAND practicing physicians, arranged alphabetically under States; and further, embraces the following:—

Lists of Officers of all regular Medical Societies in the United States.
Lists of Medical Officers of the Army and Navy, with their stations.
History and Geography of each State and Territory.
Mineral Springs of the United States, with *analyses* of their waters, and remarks on the diseases for which they are adapted.
Medical INSTITUTIONS of the several States—as Hospitals, Colleges, Infirmaries.
Medical Laws of each State, giving the requirements for practicing medicine in the several commonwealths. *This indispensable collation cannot be found elsewhere.*

The SECOND EDITION of this important work has been prepared at great cost of time and money. The lists have been carefully revised *by leading medical men in each State.* The officers of Medical Societies are those for the current year. Nearly TEN THOUSAND new names have been added, and numerous corrections made. Those who have purchased the first edition will find this one to possess *all the value of a new work.*

MODERN THERAPEUTICS, MEDICAL AND SURGICAL.

By George H. Napheys, A.M., M.D., etc. A Compendium of Recent Formulæ, Approved Treatment and Specific Methods in Medicine and Surgery. With an Appendix on Hypodermic Medication, Inhalation, Aeration, and other Remedial Agents and Therapeutic Methods of recent introduction. Fourth Edition. One Vol., large octavo, 608 pages, tinted paper. Price, mailed post-paid to any address, cloth $4.00; leather $5.00.

This work is devoted to the *Treatment of Disease* as set forth by the most eminent living physicians and surgeons, nearly 600 of whom are quoted, giving their therapeutics and *exact prescriptions.* Nearly 2,000 formulæ are given, not hackneyed recipes, but those in actual use by the greatest masters of the healing art. Many of these have never heretofore been published.

This book is a library in itself. Nearly every physician who sees it says it is "just what he wants." It includes all branches of medicine and surgery, and has three full indexes, one of authors, the second of remedies, the third of diseases. Hence it is unequalled as a book of ready reference for the busy practitioner.

The medical press has spoken of it in flattering terms, but we prefer to give the opinions of those who have actually bought it:

One purchaser writes: "It is the best investment in medical literature I ever made." Another: "It is an invaluable guide." A third: "I call it by far the most useful book in my library." A fourth: "I never had a book that gives better satisfaction than this one," and so on. That three large editions have already been sold is a guarantee of its solid and permanent value.

All the approved new remedies, with precise rules for employing them, will be found in its pages; and the methods of treatment by the hypodermic syringe, by inhalation, compressed and rarefied air, by diet, electricity and medicated baths, are explained and illustrated. The book disappoints no one who buys it.

Address the publisher,

D. G. BRINTON, M. D.,

115 SOUTH SEVENTH ST., PHILADELPHIA.

The two leading companion Medical Journals of the United States:

THE WEEKLY MEDICAL AND SURGICAL REPORTER,
THE HALF-YEARLY COMPENDIUM OF MEDICAL SCIENCE.

Edited and published by

D. G. BRINTON, M. D.,

115 South Seventh St., Philadelphia.

READ THIS:—On receipt of ten cents for postage, the Med. and Surg. Reporter will be sent for four weeks to any address, without charge.

I.
THE MEDICAL AND SURGICAL REPORTER

Is a weekly journal, issued every Saturday, in pamphlet form, bound and trimmed, containing from 22 to 26 royal octavo, double-columned pages of reading matter in each issue. It forms two large volumes annually, of over 600 pages each. It has now been established *thirty years*, and is believed to have the largest circulation of any medical journal in America.

Its special features are its *independence* and its *practicality*. It is neither the organ of any society, college, clique, or section, nor is it the advertising medium of a publishing house. Devoted to the highest and widest interests of the profession, it acknowledges no local trammels.

As it aims to be essentially *practical*, Diagnosis and Therapeutics are the branches to which it gives prominence. Hospital and Clinical Reports are sent regularly from all the leading medical centres by competent writers. The gist of the best papers read before the principal *Medical Societies* is carefully reported. *Translations* and Selections from the ablest foreign journals are constant features. As for regular *Contributors*, there is no journal with a more distinguished list. Selecting from the past year only, we may name the following: Drs. S. D. Gross, Louis A. Sayre, Jacob Da Costa, J. Marion Sims, S. Weir Mitchell, Horatio C. Wood, William Goodell, J. D. Black, Jarvis S. Wight, Wm. T. Lusk, D. Hayes Agnew, etc.

II.
THE HALF-YEARLY COMPENDIUM

Appears on January 1st and July 1st of each year, each number forming a volume of 300 large octavo pages. It contains annually from 600 to 700 carefully prepared abstracts from the periodical literature of the preceding six months from articles which have not been included in the Reporter. Thus while each journal is complete in itself, they are strictly *Companion Journals*, the one the supplement of the other.

The *Compendium* covers the whole ground of Medical Science, distributed under the following headings:

    I. Anatomy, Physiology, and Pathology.
    II. Physics, Botany, Chemistry, and Toxicology.
    III. Materia Medica and Therapeutics.
    IV. General Medicine and Sanitary Science.
    V. Clinical Medicine.
    VI. Obstetrics, and Diseases of Women and Children.
    VII. Surgery, local and general, Diseases of the Skin, etc.

A full Index accompanies each number.

The Selections are drawn from almost every medical periodical of the world; and it is the *only* such Abstract which does justice to the *American* profession.

PRICES.	PER YEAR.
The Weekly Medical and Surgical Reporter	$5.00
The Half Yearly Compendium of Medical Science	2.50
The Reporter and Compendium, *taken together*	7.00

Payable in Advance.

Thus for *seven dollars* the subscriber receives annually *four volumes* of fresh, original and carefully selected medical literature, equal to nearly 3000 pages the size of the present one.

The *Reporter* will be sent one month, four numbers, *on trial*, on receipt of 10 cents for postage. A Specimen Copy of the Compendium will be sent for $1.00.

    Address as above.

J. H. A. FOLKERS & BRO.,

Importers of

Surgical Instruments and Dental Goods,

MANUFACTURERS OF TRUSSES AND APPARATUS FOR DEFORMITIES,
Etc., DEALERS IN FINE CUTLERY.

No. 118 MONTGOMERY STREET,

San Francisco, next door to Occidental Hotel entrance.

SOLE AGENTS FOR GEO. TIEMANN & CO., NEW YORK.

Would respectfully call the attention of the Profession to our newly added excellent assortment of Electro-Medical Apparatus. We mention the celebrated

Stoehrer's Galvanic Batteries

OF 8, 16, 32 CELLS.

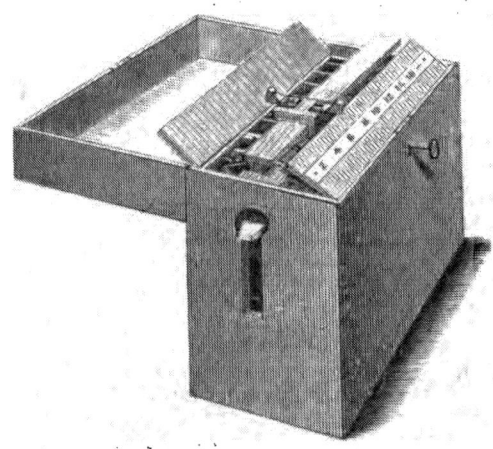

Dr. JEROME KIDDER'S ELECTRO-MEDICAL APPARATUS
GALVANO-FARADIC MF'G CO.'S APPARATUS,
CHAS. F. SMITH APPARATUS,
GAIFFE'S APPARATUS, Two Sizes,
RHUMKORFF'S APPARATUS,
DUBOIS-REYMOND APPARATUS,

TOGETHER WITH

ALL THE LATEST IMPROVED ELECTRODES.

Special Attention paid to the Manufacturing of

☞ Apparatus for Deformities and Trusses. ☜

Being in constant communication with New York, Berlin and Paris, we have all the latest improvements in this line.

J. H. A. FOLKERS & BRO.,

118 Montgomery Street, S. F.

Printed by Libri Plureos GmbH in Hamburg, Germany